Princess Affirmations

Written by Aisha

Illustrated by Valeria Leonova

Hey Princess,

Today and everyday going forward, we stand up to bullying, overshadow hate with love, embrace everything that we are and claim everything we want to become.

Love,

Aisha

Bad situations will not cause me to have bad

behavior because I am in control of my

success and take responsibility for my mistakes.

I WAS BORN TO LEAD.

TODAY, I DREAM BIGGER THAN I DID YESTERDAY.

The word "can't" is not apart of my vocabulary.

I am not too young to start making my dreams come true.

If I can dream it,

I can have it.

I am a positive influence on my friends, and

my friends are a positive influence on me.

I LOVE the skin I am in.

ONE DAY THE WORLD WILL KNOW

MY NAME.

I will learn something new today.

I bring light into every room

I enter.

I AM LOVED.

I am enough.

I will always be enough.

Hey, Pretty Girl!

I make myself proud.

I am unforgettable.

I am history
in the making.

I am a genius.

I am destined for greatness.

I am a trendsetter.

I am fearless.

My energy is contagious.

I am a legend.

I am a mogul.

My smile makes other people smile.

I am an honor roll student.

Nothing is out of my reach.

I LOVE MYSELF... A LOT.

I have billion dollar ideas.

I am confident.

EACH DAY IS ANOTHER DAY TO DO SOMETHING GREAT.

I am adventurous.

I was created

to create.

Everything I need, I have.

Everything I want,

I am working for.

My natural hair is everything!

My growing body

is beautiful.

I am a good friend and sister.

I am a thoughtful daughter.

I ATTRACT POSITIVITY.

The weird things I do are what

make me special.

I was born for a purpose.

I ignore all negativity.

I am not alone.

I belong here.

My opinions matter.

My feelings are valid.

There are no limits to what

I can accomplish.

I live in the overflow.

R E L A X !

Stress does not live here.

I am ok with asking for help when I need it. Asking for help does not mean I am weak.

I trust myself.

I am actively working
toward my goals.

I write down my goals, dreams, visions and business plans.

I choose purpose over popularity.

I have high standards and expectations for myself and those around me.

I break records.

I am the new stereotype.

I ENCOURAGE MY

BROTHERS AND SISTERS.

I always do my best.

EVERYDAY, I WALK IN MY PURPOSE, AND I AM FOCUSED ON THINGS THAT MATCH THAT PURPOSE.

This book belongs to _____

www.ingramcontent.com/pod-product-compliance
Lightning Source LLC
Chambersburg PA
CBHW040748020526
44118CB00041B/2805